D1708654

Free Papers:

*poems inspired by
the testimony of Eliza Winston,
a Mississippi slave freed in Minnesota in 1860*

poems by

Mary Moore Easter

Finishing Line Press
Georgetown, Kentucky

Free Papers:

*poems inspired by
the testimony of Eliza Winston,
a Mississippi slave freed in Minnesota in 1860*

ACKNOWLEDGMENTS

My gratitude to the publications in which these poems first appeared:

South Florida Poetry Journal [SoFloPoJo] Commodity; Up the River, Way Up
from Shiloh Plantation, Mississippi to St. Anthony Falls, Minnesota; I Look for
Her Footprints by the Mississippi River; Documentation in the Courtroom,
but None of Her Life Before; She Wasn't Prepared to Meet a Mob
The Christian Century: In My Extremity

Mary Moore Easter is a fiscal year 2020 recipient of an Artist Initiative grant
from the Minnesota State Arts Board. This activity is made possible by the
voters of Minnesota through a grant from the Minnesota State Arts Board,
thanks to a legislative appropriation by the Minnesota State Legislature; and by
a grant from the National Endowment for the Arts.

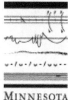

MINNESOTA
STATE ARTS BOARD

Publisher: Leah Huete de Maines
Editor: Christen Kincaid
Cover Art: nile/pixaby.com
Author Photo: Mary Ellen Frame
Cover Design: Elizabeth Maines McCleavy

Printed in the USA on acid-free paper.
Order online: www.finishinglinepress.com
         also available on amazon.com

Author inquiries and mail orders:
Finishing Line Press
P. O. Box 1626
Georgetown, Kentucky 40324
U. S. A.

Table of Contents

Excerpts from the Testimony of Eliza Winston
Appealing for Freedom, 1860

My name is Eliza Winston, am 30 years old. I was held as the slave of Mr. Gholson of Memphis, Tennessee, having been raised by Mr. Macklemo, father in law of Mr. Gohlson. I married a free man of color who hired my time of my master, who promised me my freedom upon payment of $1,000. My husband and myself worked hard and he invested our savings in a house and lot in Memphis, which was held for us in Mr. Gholson's name.

My husband by request, went out with a company of emancipated slaves to Liberia and was to stay two years. When he returned, my master was to take our house and give me my free papers, my husband paying the balance due, in money. My husband died in Liberia, and my master Mr. Gohlson got badly broken up in money matters, and having pawned me to Col. Christmas for $800, died before he could redeem me. I was never sold. I will say also that I have never received one cent from my property at Memphis since my husband died.

They have often told me I should have my freedom and they at last promised me that I should have my free papers when their child was seven years old. This time came soon after we left home to come to Minnesota. I had not much confidence that they would keep their promise for my mistress has always been feeble and she would not be willing to let me go. But I had heard that I should be free by coming to the North, and I had with my colored friends made all the preparations which we thought necessary.

After I got to St. Anthony, Minnesota, I got acquainted with a colored person and asked her if there were any persons who would help me in getting my freedom. I told her my whole story and she promised to speak with some persons about it. She did so and a white lady living near met me at the residence of my colored friend, I also told her my story and she told me there were those who would receive me and protect me. I wanted my master to give me free papers so that I could go back to Memphis where I could get employment as a nurse girl, and could earn from ten to fifteen dollars a month, and could marry there as I desire to do, but I despaired of getting my freedom in this way and although I am sorry I must sacrifice so much still I feel that if I cannot have my freedom without, I am ready to make the sacrifice.

Request for Help

[1]

I can't be the only one
who didn't notice the Universe
warning at every step,
ground creeping apart, sea rising,
plates of passage sliding shut.
I was not foolish to ignore them, just persistent.
So the slam of cymbals that froze my world
surprised me. Worse: the mute
to a silence without echo.

Nothing breathed, no pulse of blood
no sap drip, no stone rolled.
Instinct flared, no fight
only blind flight pressing into the past
breaking the seal of the present.

[2]

When you can't go forward
healing is in the past
the old folks used to say.

I grappled for the gone bodies,
slippery spirits toppling in flailing mist.
I fumbled the air
for some one of them
to right (write!) me.

Known to be indifferent
when inflicting pain,
the Universe poured forth mercy on me
in black abundance:

       Eliza is my gift to you
       Eliza's trembling heart is my gift for you
       Eliza's risk is my gift for you
       Eliza's courage is my gift for you
       Eliza's open eye is my gift to you.

In My Extremity

There you were, Eliza,
        gold from God in plain sight.

No one had picked you up
        wiped the muck from the landscape of your face.

Gold, I tell you, left for me to find,
        to polish. I won't say to own—

we've had enough of that.

I'm no colonizer of your shores,
        no conqueror to whom you must submit,

rather, a mirror that reflects what it sees—
        the you that was me, the background that was your time

the spaces surrounding you where I'd rummage
        and find my own things.

Only grace could have offered
        this circumstance to me:

the overlooked coin of the realm, a prize
        for the one who picks it up,

recognizes a value previously unimagined.
        I feel anointed by the discovery of you

a realm at the beck and call of all that is fertile in me,
        my feet untethered to walk your fields

climb the mountains
        embossed under the black of your golden face.

The old folks would shout: *Do! Jesus!*

The Message I Redact From Court Papers

free papers

my freedom

my freedom

free   my freedom

my freedom

freedom

ELIZA {X} WINSTON
her mark

In the Words of Her Mouth, a Sermon Is Made

Sisters and Brothers,

the message this morning is taken from
the Testimony of Eliza in the Book of Ancestors.
Her story in the words of her mouth
has a lot to tell us about ourselves
in this day, far from her day.

Sisters and Brothers,

bow your heads and prepare your hearts
to hear this woman speak to you
from the past.

Hear her say:

> *My name is Eliza Winston*

Testify, Eliza, testify. We hear you.

> *I am 30 years old*

Tell the truth. Eliza is a full-grown woman
Not a child. She say

> *Held as the slave of . . .*

May the slave owner's name not be called
to keep us safe from his sin!
Amen? Amen!

> *I married a free man of color*

She say she was a slave. But she say
she was also a married woman, joined
by her choice to a man of the free tribe.

She telling us that even back in that day
and in that place,
they didn't have to be of the same tribe
and condition to make a bond.
To make a bond.
She say this free man

hired my time of my master

Y'all hear this?
In the language of the day
this means a free black man paid her owner
for her labor to make her time free.
Hallelujah!

Y'all don't hear me. This upstanding man
didn't just come with pretty words.
He was a man of action.
He paid for the work she did
for someone else
to free her of obligation.
Hallelujah!

Look into yourself and see
if you can find that commitment.
Do you have that in you?
Eliza tells y'all to think on it!

My husband and myself worked hard

They toiled side by side,
one free, the other's freedom on layby.

And he invested our savings in a house and lot

Put aside your shares for the future.
Squander not your sheaves.
Take your lesson from Eliza's mouth.

The house was rented for $8 per month

Rejoice, Sisters and Brothers, rejoice
in the bounty of the Lord
for him that doeth good things.

But trouble was on the horizon
and dark clouds gathered.

My husband died in Liberia

Far from the soil of home
far from his wife, his shelter,
a stranger in a strange land.

My master pawned me for $800

She say he "pawned" her, like a diamond bracelet
like a fine vase, like a farm tool
with blood in its veins
with a promise of repayment.

And died before he could redeem me
I was never sold

Eliza, passed from hand to hand
from generation to generation
with no one to *hire her time* for her labor.

But do not despair, say the prophets,
in the darkest hour do not despair.
Do not hide the light of yourself
under a bushel. Let your goodness
shine forth. Eliza say:

> *I have always been faithful*
> *and no master I have ever had*
> *has found fault with me*

Right alongside her goodness
the light of freedom was burning in Eliza
and shining forth too. No master
or mistress could see it
because they never imagined it there
in a black woman, a pawned thing.

But shout Hallelujah for Eliza
and join in the singing of the old song
come down from our ancestors
—Hymnal # 342—
Oh freedom, oh freedom
Before I'd be a slave
I'd be buried in my grave
And go home to my Lord
And be free.

AMEN. AMEN.

Free Swagger

Jim they called him
in all his free swagger, comin round to see me
and me, sneakin a moment
between the kitchen and the back door
to hear this Jim,
Hmm-hm,
to say something to this Jim who keep comin round
when I fetch the kettle for Mistress' toddy
when I leave off the linen
from Mistress' sickroom.

I saw myself when words
took over from just lookin
and pushed silence away.
I saw myself not by myself
with this Jim, *Jim Winston*, he say
who keep coming round
with his free swagger,
gon buy you free he say.

That man got some nerve, gon buy me free.
And he think he know how! Got a plan.
And I know how.
And it's us now, not me by myself.
Don't you say there ain't no roses in my life.

Commodity 1

Investment Detail:
> *Eliza Winston*
> *30 years old*
> *held as the slave of _____*
> *having been raised by_____*
> *married a free man of color*

Contract:
> *who hired my time of my master*
> *who promised me my freedom*
> *upon payment of $1000.*
> *My husband and myself worked hard*
> *savings in a house and lot*
> *which was held for us*
> *in _____'s name.*
> *This house was rented for $8 per month.*

Transaction Detail:
> *My master was to take our house*
> *and give me my free papers,*
> *my husband paying the balance due*
> *in money.*
> *My husband died*
> *My master having pawned me for $800*
> *died before he could redeem me.*
> *I was never sold.*

Change in Account Value:
> *I went with my young mistress.*
> *I became the slave of _____*
> *seven years ago last March.*
> *They told me*
> *I should have my free papers*
> *when their child was seven years old.*
> *not much confidence*
> *they would keep their promise.*
> *She would not be willing to let me go*

Reinvest/Rollover:
> *I should be free by coming to the North...*

Commodity 2

Held as the slave of having been raised by hired my time of my master payment of $1000 take our house and give me my free papers paying the balance due in money pawned me for $800 before he could redeem me never sold became the slave of held as the slave of having been raised by hired my time hired my time of my master payment of $1000 payment of $1000 take our house and give me my free papers paying the balance due in money balance due in money pawned me for $800 pawned me for $800 before he could redeem me never sold became the slave of held as the slave hired my time payment of $1000 take our house balance due in money pawned me for $800 before he could redeem me never sold never sold never sold became the slave of held as the slave of $1000 $800 balance due in money balance due in moneybalance due in money balance due in money

Those Who Made Two Years' Worth of Her Clothes Tell about It

[1]

Hear tell the land would be white
in winter.
Hear tell the white would be soft
as cotton
with thorns of ice
not growing from the ground
but falling from the sky.
Hear tell what she gon need
for a body used to heat.
I make a secret round my waist
of Mistress' ripped pantaloons
stolen honey-cover
smuggled down the slave line
ripped at will.
She won't miss its rent
unmended.
Plenty more where that come from.

[2]

As long as these old fingers hold a thimble
you will not tremble in whatever cold
they have for you, Eliza.
You are not motherless without cover
in your solitude. Take with you this vest
with sleeves, stitched and doubled, cotton-stuffed
these skirts and sack shirts closed with pilfered buttons
tagged with bits of cut-off ribbon
to remind your joy to rise
inside your obedient face
your fire to blaze inside
whatever cold they have for you.
Take us with you in each fold and pleat
armored by the freedom that you seek.

Up the River, Way Up from Shiloh Plantation, Mississippi to St. Anthony Falls, Minnesota

In droves they came.
They left the heat behind
the Mississippi musk and heavy air.
A change of scene would do them good
the Falls and water rushing free in foam.

They took their comforts with them:
cook who kept the south inside their mouths
slave who'd sleep on floor outside their door
waked at any whim or need
the hand that held the sickly head
and kept the children out of mind,
that hefted, smoothed and scurried, dark
as nighttime in the day, invisible,
a nothing to imagine with a plan.

Eliza came, was brought along,
to hold the sickly head.
She left the bondage of her home behind,
left friends who knew her leaving was for good
and kept her plan for freedom sealed,
left musk and heavy air and duties owned
by those whose promises betrayed her trust.

She did her *very best*, a comfort to herself
her standard steady over churning water
her forward motion out of sight beneath
the flashing surface of the paddleboat.
She smoothed and scurried *closely confined*
by minutes, hours, days, nights
waiting to alight on land, free land.

I Look for Her Footprints by the Mississippi River

By 1937 this stretch of stone and sand
was Lambert's Landing, the original shore
dredged to make Warner Road
where my car noses into a cul-de-sac
full of today's stone mills, train rails and storage tanks.
Where are Eliza's footprints?

The Dakota named the shore here
I-mni-za ska dan or "little white rocks."
Sandstone bluffs loomed high and white over the water.
Later, immigrants called it
the Lower Landing at St. Paul
where steamships unloaded them onto the dock
and into new lives.

Slave-owner tourists from the south
weren't looking for new lives.
They didn't guess one of their possessions
was planning for it, never to return
to this dock, never this ship going
downriver for days to be moored
in the fettered place called home.

Eliza went down the gangplank
to land that would be her freedom soon,
her foot touching soil—here? —
before the railroads came
with their tracks and switchers.
Above the bluffs, Indian mounds lay quiet
as they had for centuries.

Not free yet, she steadied the arm
of her mistress through the bustling port
on the river's second big bend.

Passengers on four hundred boats a day
rode a Mississippi as mighty then as now
when this very March the river crested at 19 feet,
flooding green acres of park and parkland signs.

Not free yet, not free yet,
the chant she held to her heart
as tight as the hand of the child she raised
to climb into the surrey sent for them, no footprints.
Not free yet as they rocked up the hill
from waterside to the top of present-day Jackson Street.
She chanted its motion on the ride
to the hotel elegance of Winslow House.

With the magnificent view of St. Anthony waterfalls
demanding all attention, who would notice Eliza's footprints
on Cheever's Landing. Only a mile upriver
until the end of their long water journey.
Not free yet. Quick, the cart!

Winslow House in St. Anthony: A Script for Three Voices

Eliza: Winslow House, the Big House in the North
          five stories tall, curved bannisters, silk drapes
          nothing new to me except the soil it sets on
          is free soil not the slave dirt of the delta
          holding the bones of a stranger
          who looked a side eye at me once—my mother?
          then quick drew her gaze back to the hoe,
          whip-bent and staring down that handle into her grave.
          Winslow House, masters and slaves on every floor,
          mistresses and the maids they own to dress them.

Poet: My grandmother was a maid and nanny.

Grandmother Moore:
          I was never owned. I served for good pay.

Eliza: I had a house once

Poet: Me, too, Eliza. Me, too.

Eliza: *and a lot we invested our savings in.*
          This house was rented for $8 per month.

Grandmother Moore:
          little cottage seaside, mine.

Poet: When I was four, Grandma, the sea there, on my ankles.

Eliza: I had a husband once—

Poet: Me, too, Eliza. Twice.

Eliza: man with a plan to buy me free,

Grandmother Moore:
          Mine was never owned either. He served for pay
          driving that big car far away.

Eliza: man with a view from the big world . . .

Poet: I wanted to walk in the big world.

Eliza: Hush, you two. It's my story to tell. Go away.
         . . . to the world in our house
         two backs bent to the work, bent to the laws
         that gave Master the holding
         along with a promise he never could keep.
         Death, you know, kept the secret of his failure.

         Jim, they called my husband. Jim, I said, my choice.

Grandmother Moore:
         My son, Jim!

Poet: Jim, my father!

Eliza: I said, Hush!
         Jim was free. Master took his money for my labor.
         A man used to traveling, *my husband by request, went out*
         with a company of emancipated slaves to Liberia
         and was to stay two years. Eight dollars per month
         by one year is ninety-six dollars.
         Eight dollars per month by two years amounts to
         one hundred and ninety-two dollars
         of my labor earned toward my freedom.
         My husband died in Liberia and I was pawned
         to pay my Master's debts but never sold free.
         Death kept the measure of his failure.

         I have never received one cent from my property
         at Memphis since my husband died,

         a free man with a house we would own . . .

Poet and Grandmother Moore:
      We would own . . .

Eliza: . . . never stayed at Winslow House,
      slaves and masters on every floor.

Records in the Courtroom, but None of Her Life Before

for all of us who come from people who signed with X's
—Danez Smith

[1]

Someone took it down,
their sworn duty to record every word,
only one sign of her sound: *Macklemo*
explained in parentheses (Macklemore)
the tongue of her region, her status,
her origin outside taught English.
No further apostrophe or dropped consonant to interfere
with eloquence and flow, like she could—even back then,
especially back then in the X-signed days—
could rap and roll out her life with all its twists, turns
and switchbacks; indignation in the unsaid
another-thing-while-I'm-at-it
I will say also I have never received one cent
from my property in Memphis . . .
talkback poking through a retort
to couldawouldashoulda freedom promises
Why didn't you give it in St. Louis—
someone took it down and her voice lived
right into my ear.

[2]

No one took down Eliza at five years old, at four,
at her mother's breast or some other breast
assigned to keep her alive when her mother's birth body
gave out, worn out, worn down to its last act of giving her breath.

Nothing documents the opposite, a mother's shield
in the early days tied to her back,
first steps, the surprise of quick speech,
the shush of her tongue in danger.

No one took down which loss cemented her concept of self
held as slave of Mr. Gholson, raised by Mr. Macklemo
instead of daughter of—what name goes here, Eliza?—
born of a woman like every one of us who draws breath and turns
to ashes,
born of a woman, flesh of her flesh, the one-made-two
at first inhale of a world. What name?

[3]

Macklemore, Gholston, Christmas,
Babbitt, Bigelow, King,
Vanderburgh: around her
names and histories abound
wives and progeny and property
in records and deeds and diaries
and newspapers and courtrooms
and censuses and street addresses
and cemeteries and votes
Eliza—a flame blown out
leaving smoke
and the burnt end of a paper.

Character Witness for Herself

I married a free man of color
My husband and myself worked hard
I have always been faithful and no master that I have ever had has found
fault with me
I thought I had a right to my clothes because they did not come from my
master or mistress
I minded her
I told him I was not going to do wrong
I have always been faithful to him and done my best to please him and
my mistress.
I have been closely confined
I have never fretted or complained because I thought if I did my very best,
they would perhaps give me my freedom.
I would not marry anyone but a free person
I could go back to Memphis where I could get employment as a nurse girl,
and could earn from ten to fifteen dollars a month
I am sorry I must sacrifice so much
I am ready to make the sacrifice.
I prefer freedom.

When I Was Told I Was Free

my Mistress's why?

I was told I was free

my Master's offer of ten dollars to go with him

I was free

my sacrifice

free

A forming nation found me wrong
an instigation to unrest   *free*   a prod
to catalyze a courtroom, city

I was free

whole economy, a test of money lost (theirs)

I was told I was free

and freedom won (mine) that left me fleeing
still the mob outside the courtroom, their anger

When I was told I was free

as they turned their empty pockets out.

She Wasn't Prepared to Meet a Mob

Eliza didn't expect roses and sunshine
Where in her life had there ever been roses?
Still she wasn't prepared to meet a mob
at the threshold of the courtroom
place of triumph—FREE!
FREE to walk into arms raised against her,
shouts bursting above an angry murmur
malign intent simmering in the air.
Her guardians grasped her arms,
hustled her to a carriage.
She gasped in the gallop of hooves
away to a big house
away to clamor at the door, crowd gathering outside.
In the simmer, she stood FREE in the stairwell.
When they battered the door
she stood FREE as the lady of the house leveled her pistol
and fired a shot that backed them away.
All night the mob would not have it, this FREEdom
that damaged their purses. Resistance lurked
in the air. Protectors whisked her farther away
under a cloak? in a disguise? Fear rattling her free chest.
Steady pulse to sustain her.
How far away was FREEdom and rest?

What Comes Now?

Lawd, I'm out here on your word, a plea each time
she was set to hide in the wood
waiting for rescue to find her.

Lawd, I'm out here on your word,
a reminder of promises, a compact for faith met
with courage inside risk,
words forced from her lips by uncertainty
borrowed from others who looked for hope in despair
while she bided her time alone.

No way she knew to say
"I celebrate myself" and yet she did.
She could not say what hadn't been written yet:
"come celebrate/ with me
that everyday/ something has tried to kill me/
and has failed."

She took "(her) one hand holding tight/ (her) other hand;"
and set out not without regret
in clear pursuit of what most thought
she couldn't win or didn't deserve to get.

Hers was the year Clothilde, the last slave ship,
sneaked into anchor and was set afire
to hide the crime, disgorging
a hundred Africans onto land where they met
the very bondage she would not accept.

She could not see six months ahead
a nation split, half willing to forget
the principles that bound them,
half standing up to pay a debt
to stolen men and women.
She did not know the details
of the world that swirled around her world.
She took off anyway on the roiling surface
of the wet river, her deed stretching out
in unseen time and space.

I Take to Dreaming of Her Future

If Eliza lived twenty free years
surely not *a nurse girl* in Memphis.
Memphis was burning, Memphis
was killing freed blacks in sweeping riots.
Memphis had no place for her plans
the other side of Emancipation.

If Eliza lived twenty free years
might she have heard news of *the child of my mistress*
I have taken care of from her birth to the present
I am so attached to the child that I would be willing
to serve. . .
Would some mother's instinct have shivered her bones
when that child, now bride
married a titled Frenchman in Paris?
Would that treasured child
long for the touch on her veil
of Eliza's mothering hand
at the moment of her social ascent
or would her sweet memory be of
"my old mammy down South."
    "Give me the child until (s)he is seven
        and I will show you the (wo)man"

If Eliza lived for twenty free years
(She might have, people survived
to fifty's old age)
she would have overlapped a life
with my grandmother,
mere babe of the 1880s squalling
toward her own destiny
in a world the other side of Emancipation.

If Eliza lived twenty free years
what past clung tightly to her, what plan
dropped from her shoulders
and was trod to dust?

Timeline: Through Eliza, I Chart My Family

The dates in recorded history
of Eliza's appearances
light a crisscross of connections,
a constellation in which my own ancestors shine—
women who bore their servitude
in the dark of her skyscape—

1830: Eliza is born

1843: My great-grandmother Anna Mallory is born on Christmas day.

Eliza is thirteen this year, still hidden
in the unknown. Anna's mother's written trace has been erased
but unlike Eliza, Anna knew her mother and passed
her name down the future line: Margaret Mallory

1853: Eliza, at 23-years old, pawned to her second master, emerges
into her own recorded story.

Eliza begins caring for the master's newborn.
My great-grandma Anna was ten, not yet at puberty, not yet
aware.

1856: Eliza continues care for the master's child while
Anna learns the way she is plucked and picked
at thirteen-years-old, to carry her master's child
in her body toward delivery of Horace Mallory.

(Horace will leave home with a stranger in Lawrenceville at age
12.
Horace who never returned or was found.
Someone took it down.)

Trapped by life's stranglehold,
where could a child with a child outrun slavery?)

Every woman knows how personal circumstance
slams the door on—which way to run, and where,
children: how to take them along, how to leave them behind,
how to keep them alive.

(Anna will bear her first master three children.)

1860: Eliza secures free papers

1863: In captivity, Anna gives birth again, to Nora Mallory.
Born two years after Eliza's escape,
she's called SuhNora, (Sister Nora) by her siblings

Margaret Mallory: Ain Mag (named after her grandmother
Margaret) who'd come to visit and stay for a month,
reading everyone's mail if they didn't hide it.

Eliza lived with unkept promises until she devised
a blazing moment in the record for all to see freedom's face.
And then she receded into a free anonymity.
I can't find her anywhere beyond the horizon of Emancipation.

1871: My great-grandmother Anna Mallory's star in the
constellation falls
into her second master. Sold, bartered, taken-in
though legally free in 1871 said Lincoln (not the plantation)
she keeps the name she has earned with three Mallory
children in a new place, new master.

1876: At 33 years old Anna birthed her fourth baby:
the Turnbull master's child that would be my grandmother,
Hardie Turnbull, born free.

1878: Clarence Turnbull was born of Anna. He's Hardie's Lil Brother.
Hardie reported to my childhood ears that folks said
of her and her brother:

>   "I declare, those children look more like Robert Turnbull
>   than his own children."
The other children called Hardie "ole reddy fox" because of her
red hair that confirmed by resemblance her young master was
their father.
Hardie told my curiosity: "All my people gone on away from
here."

1879:   This is Eliza's nineteenth year of freedom.
        Someone takes my ancestor's told stories down
        in the front of the Bible.
        Anna has a third father for Kate Wilkes, the last of her five
        children.

1892:   The constellation grows when Hardie married James William
        Smith.
        This was the time when the white child Eliza cared for was
        married in Paris.

1895:   My grandmother Hardie Turnbull's story endures.
        Her first two children die as toddlers. Then Clarence William
        Smith, named for her Lil Brother and her husband, is born in
        1895.

1898:   Anna's grandbaby Eunice Wilkes Smith comes into the world
        in 1898, and Anna goes out. When my great-grandmother dies
        this year, is Eliza alive for her 38th year of freedom?
        This is unanswerable, unknown.

        Undine Anna Smith, my mother with her middle name
        for her Grandmother Anna is born 1904.

        And Anna's trail finds its way down the generations to me.

She Is Here Now

Eliza steps out from the erasure
of slavery to leave words
in a court document
that blaze a light
and bristle a world.
I refuse her utter blankness
after she seizes freedom.

Although she became free,
as a black woman,
she had nowhere to go, no one to care
once her drama served
their principles.
Unlikely we will find her *a nurse girl in Memphis.*
Memphis was burning.

Don't let her go!
Find her here now.
Her courage ignites our courage.
Keep her risk inside our risk.
Let's see the world
out of her open eyes.
Hear her outspoken voice in our own mouths.
Go from these pages
to a freedom she cedes to you.
and you
and you.

Notes and Bibliography

Greene, Wm D. "Eliza Winston and the Politics of Freedom in Minnesota 1854-60," *Minnesota History* 57, no. 3, (Fall 2000)
"Col. Richard Christmas, the wealthy planter from Issaquena County, Mississippi, arrived in St. Anthony in August1860. He had never brought slaves on his vacations in the North because of what he had heard about abolition activities, but in the summer of1860 his wife was too ill to travel without her slave's assistance." Thus Eliza Winston accompanied them. [Shiloh plantation had 166 slaves.]

————"The Summer Christmas Came to Minnesota: The Case of Eliza Winston, a Slave." *Law and Inequality: A Journal of Theory and Practice 8*, no. 1 (November 1989)

Eliza Winston's Account of Her Case, Minnesota Historical Society, Document, 1860
Eliza Winston Court Case, MNOPEDIA, http://www.mnopedia.org/event/eliza-winston-cour-case
Shaw, Madelyn, "Slave Cloth and Clothing Slaves: Craftsmanship, Commerce, and Industry"
The Issaquena Genealogy and History Project, The Richard Christmas Family
Potter, Merle, 101 Best Stories of Minnesota,
Zalusky, Joseph, Winslow House Register, Hennepin County History, Spring 1967

I wish to acknowledge the contributions of the Gale Family Library at the Minnesota Historical Society; and the Minnesota African American Heritage Museum and Gallery.

Hunter, Tera W., New York Times (@TeraWHunter)
"On April 16, 1862, President Abraham Lincoln signed a bill emancipating enslaved people in Washington, the end of a long struggle. But to ease slaveowners' pain, the District of Columbia Emancipation Act paid those loyal to the Union up to $300 for every enslaved person freed." (emphasis mine)

Title: Eliza Winston's Account of Her Case
Type: Document
Date: 1860
Source: Minnesota Historical Society

Description: Since the court records of the Eliza Winston case were never made public, people involved in the case published their opinions and interpretations of the event in the local newspapers. This is Eliza Winston's testimony in the case.

Transcription:

STATE OF MINNESOTA
Hennepin County

ELIZA WINSTON, *being duly sworn, deposes and says:*

My name is ELIZA WINSTON, am 30 years old. I was held as the slave of Mr. Gholson of Memphis, Tennessee, having been raised my Mr. Macklemo, father in law of Mr. Gohlson. I married a free man of color who hired my time of my master, who promised me my freedom upon payment of $1,000. My husband and myself worked hard and he invested our savings in a house and lot in Memphis, which was held for us in Mr. Gholson's name. This house was rented for $8 per month. My husband by request, went out with a company of emancipated slaves to Liberia, and was to stay two years. He went out with them because he was used to travelling, and it was necessary to have some one to assist and take care of them. When he returned, my master was to take our house and give me my free papers, my husband paying the balance due, in money. My husband died in Liberia, and my master Mr. Gohlson got badly broken up in money matters, and having pawned me to Col. Christmas for $800, died before he could redeem me. I was never sold. I have always been faithful and no master that I have ever had has found fault with me. Mr. Macklemo my first master always treated me kindly and has tried to buy me of Col. Christmas, a good many times. When Mr. Gholson married Mr. Macklemo's daughter, I went with my young mistress. I became the slave of Mr. Christmas seven years ago last March. They have often told me I should have my freedom and they at last promised me that I should have my free papers when their child was seven years old. This time came soon after we left home to come to Minnesota. I had not much confidence that they would keep their promise for my mistress has always been feeble and she would not be willing to let me go. But I had heard that I should be free by coming to the North, and I had with my colored friends made all the preparations which we thought necessary, I had got a little money and spent it in clothes, my colored friends gave me some good clothing, and I came away with a good supply of clothing in my trunk, sufficient to last me two years and of a kind suitable to what we supposed this climate would be. The trunk containing this clothing was left at the Winslow House when we went to Mrs. Thornton's, I taking only one calico dress, besides and old washing dress. After I got to St. Anthony, I got acquainted with a colored person and asked her if there were any persons who would help me in getting my freedom. I told her my whole story and she promised to speak with some persons about it. She did so and a white lady living near met me at the residence of my colored friend, I also told her my story and she told me there were those who would receive me and protect me. I thought I had a right to my clothes because they did not come from my master or mistress and I purposed to carry away at different times when I should not be suspected, some portion of them. I fixed upon the coming Sunday when I would leave my master, but before the time came Col. Christmas and his family went out to Mrs. Thornton's and as I understood were not coming back to the Winslow House to stay any more, I thought some one of the servants had made my master suspicious and that he went away on that account. On the day I was taken by the officer, some men came out to Mrs. Thornton's, and I heard them tell them that persons were coming out to carry me off. So whenever any one was seen coming, my mistress would send me into the woods at the back of the house, I minded her, but I did not go very far hoping they would find me. I was sent into the woods several times during the day, as was the case at the time when the party came who took me away. I had on my washing dress and I went into change it before going with the officer. My mistress asked me why I went off in this way, she said she would give me free papers, I asked her why she did not in St. Louis. She said over again and again that I must not go in this way but that they would give me my free papers. I told her I had rather go now. When my master came into the court room he came up to me and gave me ten dollars. When I was told I was free my master asked me if I would go with him, told me not to do wrong. I told him I was not going to do wrong, but that I did not wish to go with him. I have been Col. Christmas' slave for more than seven years, and I have always been faithful to him and done my best to please him and my mistress. The latter has always been feeble and I have waited upon her and taken care of her and the child. During all this time, owing to the poor health of my mistress, I have been closely confined, have had scarcely any time to myself or to see the other slaves, as as most house servants can have, but I have never fretted or complained because I thought if I did my very best, they would perhaps give me my freedom. Since my husband died I might have married very happily with a free colored person, but Col. Christmas would not let me marry any one but one of his plantation hands, and I would not marry any one but a free person, I thought if I could not better myself by marrying I would not marry at all, and I knew it would be worse for me if I married a slave. I wanted my master to give me free papers so that I could go back to Memphis where I could get employment as a nurse girl, and could earn from ten to fifteen dollars a month, and could marry there as I desire to do, but I despaired of getting my freedom in this way and although I am sorry I must sacrifice so much still I feel that if I cannot have my freedom without, I am ready to make the sacrifice. I will say also that I have never received one cent from my property at Memphis since my husband died.

It was my own free choice and purpose to obtain my freedom, and I applied to my colored friend in St. Anthony, without solicitation on the part of any other person. I have nursed and taken care of the child of my mistress from her birth till the present, and am so attached to the child that I would be willing to serve Col. Christmas, if I could be assured of my freedom eventually, but with all my attachment to the child, I prefer freedom in Minnesota, to life long slavery in Mississippi.

ELIZA {X} WINSTON
her mark

Subscribed and sworn to before me this 24th day of Aug. A.D. 1860.
J.F. Bradley, Justice of the Peace.

Personal thanks:

Eliza Winston appeared in my life as a gift. For a short book, long thanks to the many people and institutions who helped me welcome her to the page in intense months of obsession and effort. First among these is poet Margaret Hasse who as friend and editor brought enormous experience to the smallest detail and the overall conception of the book. She read my poems with expert eye and poet's imagination, discerned my mind and guided me toward clarity for my reader on subjects that felt dangerous in other contexts. She lent support and withstood confrontation. Hers was a voice I could argue with, a leader I could follow, depart from, and follow again.

I'm fortunate to be a member of groups from whom I received valuable commentary, engagement and ongoing interest. Through the stages of research and writing, some provided the intimacy of long association; others reflected the freshness of more distant perspective. I recognize and praise Penchant (The Northfield Women Poets) my 40-year poetry group; the passionate identification with Eliza's story from the members of Twin Cities Black Women Writing; the line-by-line examination of the Ginger Poetry Workshop; the enthusiasm of the Saint Anthony Park United Church Of Christ (Victoria Wilgoki pastor) Adult Forum which gave Eliza's poems their first public outing on the way to publication.

I owe a personal debt of gratitude to my family for offering their voices to embody the words of *Free Papers*, each member taking a page round-robin style: daughters Allison Easter and Mallory Easter Polk, son-in-law Preston Polk, and grandchildren Marcus Polk, Charlotte Polk and Vanessa Polk (and across an ocean, Mason Polk).

I thank individuals who read in dialogue with me, and those who directed me to publication outlets for specific poems: Marilyn Benson, Carolyn Holbrook, Jean Ann Durades, Joan Hepburn; Minnesota-born guides Colleen Callahan and Mary Jo Thompson in research walks along Mississippi River locations infused with Eliza in the past.

In addition to *Free Papers,* **Mary Moore Easter** is the author of three other poetry books, *The Body of the World* (Minnesota Book Award in Poetry Finalist, 2019), *Walking from Origins,* and *From the Flutes of Our Bones* (2020). Her poems have been widely published in *Poetry, Prairie Schooner, The Christian Century, Water~Stone, SoFloPoJo* and others as well as several anthologies.

Born in Petersburg, Virginia, to parents on the faculty of Virginia State College (now University), Mary Moore Easter was as immersed in their artistic and intellectual interests as she was in the limitations segregation imposed on her black world. Raised in a musical household (mother, Undine Smith Moore, composer, and father, James Arthur Moore, tenor), she loved poems and the poetic voice from childhood. Her father's "Whan that Aprille," and her mother's "my heart leaps up" set her young ear. She carried this attachment to poetry through an adult career as an independent dancer/choreographer and Founder and Director of Carleton College's dance program. This fortuitous overlap of art forms led to the lasting primacy of the written word. As a Cave Canem Fellow, all inhibitions to her African American languages were flung aside.

Easter's work has been sustained by Penchant (Northfield Women Poets), Ginger Poetry Workshop with Margaret Hasse, and Twin Cities Black Women Writing. Her awards include: Artist Initiative Grant from the Minnesota State Arts Board (2020), Pushcart Prize-nomination, Bush Artist Fellowship in Choreography, multiple McKnight Awards in Interdisciplinary Arts, The Loft Literary Center's Creative Non-Fiction Award, and residencies at Ragdale and The Anderson Center. Easter holds a B.A. from Sarah Lawrence and an M.A. in Music for Dancers from Goddard.

CPSIA information can be obtained
at www.ICGtesting.com
Printed in the USA
LVHW090319080521
686829LV00001B/27